Y430
J3

First published in the U.K. 1983 by Blandford Press,
Link House, West Street, Poole, Dorset, BH15 1LL

Copyright © 1983 Blandford Books Ltd

Based on Blandford's original Very First Bible Stories,
illustrated by Treyer Evans, and others.

Co-edition arranged with the help of Angus Hudson, London.

ISBN 0 7137 1320 8

All Rights Reserved. No part of this
publication may be reproduced, stored in a
retrieval system, or transmitted, in any form
or by any means, electronic, mechanical,
photocopying, recording or otherwise,
without prior permission.

Made and printed in Italy

The Story of Samuel

By Joan Kendall

Illustrated by Patricia Papps
and Andrew Skilleter

BLANDFORD PRESS
Poole   Dorset

Once there was a woman called Hannah. She lived long ago with her husband, who loved her dearly. The only thing that made them sad was that they had no children. Hannah often prayed to God that He would send her a baby boy.

Every year they went together to the Temple to worship God. "Perhaps this year God will send me a baby," thought Hannah. "I will pray especially hard."

And this is what she said to God, "O Lord, if you will give me a son, I will give him back to you again, and he shall serve you all his life."

At the Temple there lived an old priest called Eli. He came up to Hannah and asked her what she was doing. "I am very unhappy," she told him, "I have been telling God, and I have asked Him for something very special."

"Go in peace," said Eli, "and may God give you what you have asked of Him."

Hannah was happy and went home with her husband. Sure enough, before a year had passed, God sent her a baby son. They called his name Samuel, which means, "asked of God."

Hannah taught Samuel to be helpful and obedient and, when he was old enough, his father and mother took him to the Temple.

They took a present with them—three bullocks, some flour, and a bottle of wine. Perhaps Samuel rode on one of the bullocks when he got tired.

They brought the child to Eli, and Hannah said, "Oh, Sir, I am the woman you spoke to last time I came here. I prayed for a child, and God sent me this boy. I have come to carry out my promise and give him back to God."

Then she and her husband went home again and left Samuel behind with old Eli. Samuel waved goodbye to them.

Each year Hannah made her son
a coat, and when she went to
the Temple, she took it with her
and gave it to him. How glad
they were to see each other!
How proud she was of him!

Samuel was like a son to Eli, who was now very old and going blind. Samuel kept the Temple clean, filled the oil lamps, and washed the bowls and waterpots.

Eli had two grown-up sons of his own, but they were both wicked. They did not love God nor did they try to serve Him. They would not listen to their father, and were a bad example to everyone.

25

One night Samuel helped Eli get ready for bed as usual. It was dark in the Temple and the lamp was burning low. Samuel lay down to sleep in the part of the Temple near the ark of God.

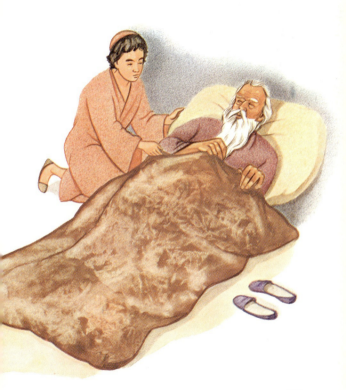

Suddenly, he heard a voice saying, "Samuel! Samuel!"

Samuel answered, "Here I am."

Then he got up and ran into Eli's room, and said, "Here I am, for you called me."

"I did not call you, my son," Eli replied. "Lie down again."

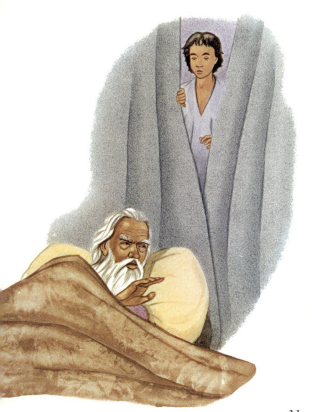

So Samuel went back to bed and lay down. Before long he heard his name called again. He jumped up and ran into Eli's room. "Here I am," he said. "You really did call me."

"I did not call you," answered Eli. "Go and lie down again."

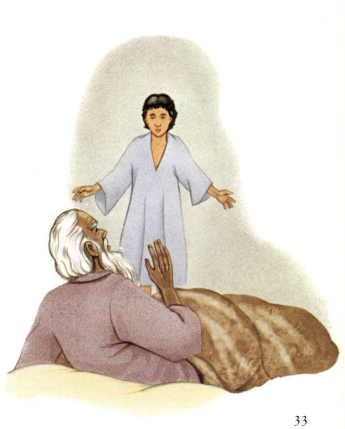

Samuel was very puzzled, but he did as he was told. Someone was calling him, and who could it be but Eli? He lay down, and for the third time he heard his name called. Up he got again and ran into Eli's room. "Master," he said, "I did hear you calling me!"

Then Eli realized it was God who wanted to speak to Samuel. "Go back once more," he told him, "and if you hear the voice again, say, 'Speak, Lord, for your servant is listening.'"

When the voice spoke his name again, Samuel remembered what Eli had told him, and said, "Speak, for your servant is listening."

God said, "I am going to bring great trouble upon Eli and his sons. I have told him many times that this would happen, because his sons do wicked things and he will not stop them."

In the morning, Eli called him and said, "Samuel, you must tell me everything that God has said to you. Do not keep anything back." Samuel did as he was told, and Eli said, "Yes, that is God speaking. He must do what He thinks is right."

Not long after this, Eli's sons were killed in battle, and the ark of God was captured. When the bad news was brought to old Eli, he fell off his chair and died.

Samuel grew up to be a man, and God was with him and often spoke to him. He obeyed God all his life, and became the leader of the people of Israel.

«This story is taken from 1 Samuel chapters 1-3».

43